HOW Does a keyboard put your words on screen?

Om KIDZ
An imprint of Om Books International

Contents

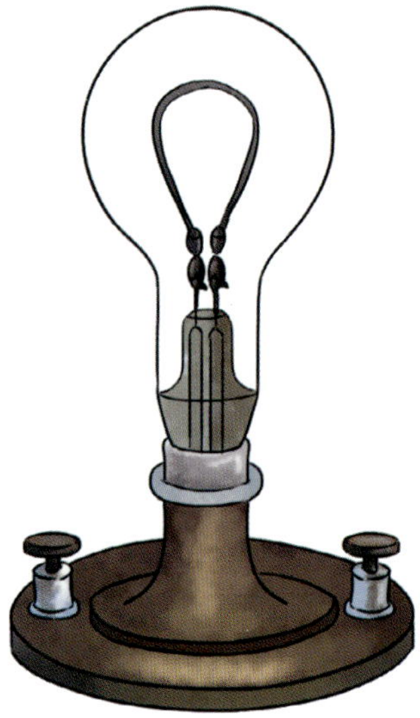

How old is the oldest invention?

It's as old as around 3 million years! The oldest inventions are said to be the most basic stone implements that were made by early humans. These include stone cores, hammer-stones, anvils and sharp stone flakes. These tools were made by hitting stones against each other, or applying pressure with wood or bones. Early men used these tools for hunting and protecting themselves.

Pocket fact

The oldest tools!
The world's oldest stone tools were discovered from the shores of Lake Turkana in Kenya, and are almost 3 million years old!

Find out

How did the ancient Greeks light a fire?

How was fire discovered?

There are several theories on how fire was discovered. Some believe that pre-humans first noticed fire after lightning struck a tree. It is said that then they must have learnt to make fire using sticks and flint. Soon, they discovered that it was possible to use fire for heat, light and cooking food.

How were wheels used in ancient times?

They first served as a potter's wheel! Wheels first appeared in Mesopotamia more than 5,000 years ago. They were initially used by potters for shaping clay. It was much later that wheels were fitted to carts, which made movement much easier.

Pocket fact

No wheels exist in nature!
Throughout history, most inventions were inspired by the natural world. The idea to invent fork came from forked sticks; the airplane from gliding birds. But the wheel was not inspired by any existing object; it was purely man's innovation.

Try this!

Name the parts of a wheel.

How is a crossbar wheel similar to the modern wheel?

It had spokes and a crossbar! The crossbar was invented after the early semi-solid wheels. It had a piece of wood called crossbar running from one side of the wheel to the other to make it stronger. It also had spokes that linked the middle of the wheel to the outer edge. It looked similar to the modern wheel, especially the wheel of a bicycle.

How old are the first writing records?

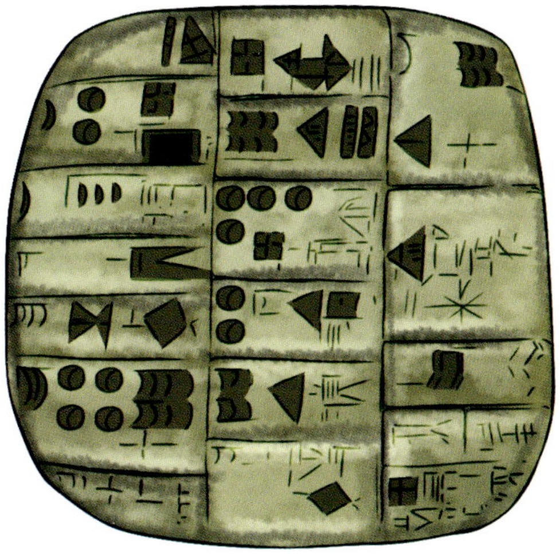

Approximately 5,000 years old! The earliest writing we know of, dates back to around 3,000 BCE and was probably invented by the Sumerians, who lived in southern Mesopotamia. However, it was much different from the present-day writing. Most early writing systems began with symbols and small images instead of words.

Pocket fact

Quill pen!
The quill, the hollow shaft of a bird's feather, was also used as a writing tool in the ancient times. It was first used as a pen in around 500 CE.

Find out

When did the alphabet first originate?

How did the first writing tool look like?

It was a pointed tool! The Sumerians are credited with the invention of the first writing tool called a 'stylus'. It was made from reed, a strong thin plant, and produced a wedge shape each time it was pressed into wet clay.

How was ink made in ancient times?

It was made of carbon! The first writing ink was invented by the Egyptians and the Chinese in 2500 BCE. It was made of carbon mixed with a solution of glue or gum and moulded into sticks. The sticks were dried but they were mixed with water before use.

Pocket fact

Not blurred anymore!
Johannes Gutenberg invented a special oil-based ink in the 1400s. This ink prevented blurry edges and adhered to Gutenberg's newly invented printing press.

Find out

What has the word "paper" been derived from?

How was paper first made?

It was made from mulberry bark! Papermaking dates back to about 105 CE, when Ts'ai Lun, an official attached to the Imperial court of China made a sheet of paper using mulberry fibres. He made it by mixing mulberry bark and other fibres with old rags, hemp waste and fishnets. He then mashed it flat, pressed out the water and let it dry in the sun.

How were calculations done in the ancient times?

It started with fingers and other objects! The first method of calculation was counting on fingers. This gradually changed to the use of tallies that were made by carving notches in wood, bone and stone. Much later the first calculating tool called the abacus came to use in Europe, China and Russia. It is believed that abacus was first used by Babylonians as early as 2400 BCE.

Pocket fact

Heaven beads!

The Chinese abacus called the Suanpan had two beads on the rods on the upper side and five beads on the rods on the lower side of the divider. The upper beads are called the heaven beads and the lower beads are called the earth beads.

Try this!

Calculate 1010010 + 1001011 with the help of a calculator. Which number did you get?

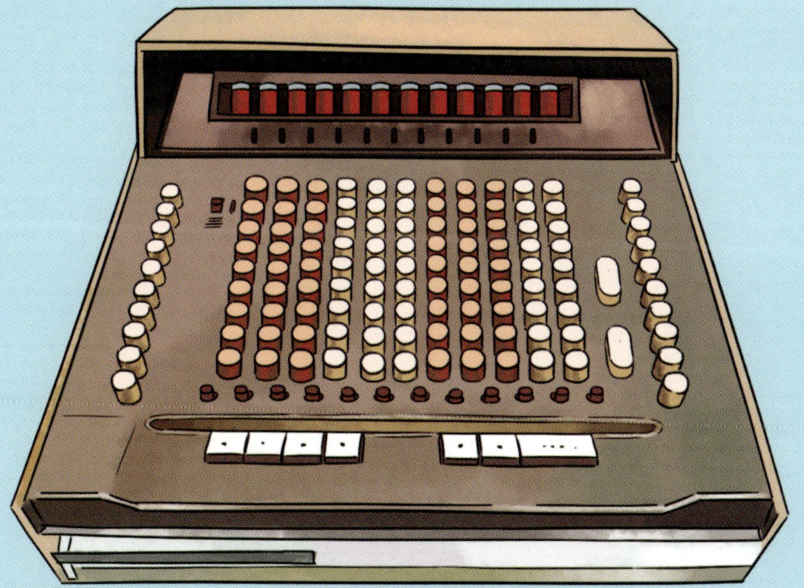

How was the first mechanical calculator invented?

It was invented using metal wheel dials! The first mechanical calculator was invented in 1642 by Blaise Pascal. It had a polished brass box, about 350 mm x 125 mm x 75 mm in dimension. There were eight movable metal dials with the numbers 0–9 that were turned to the appropriate numbers using a stylus. The answers were displayed in boxes on the top of the calculator.

How were long-distance messages sent before the invention of telephones?

They were sent using telegraphs. The telegraph was first invented in 1791 by Claude and Ignace Chappe in France. It used sound along with times on a clock face for sending messages. But it wasn't very successful. Later, in 1837, Samuel Morse developed the electric telegraph that worked by transmitting electrical signals over a wire laid between stations.

Pocket fact

The First Message!

The first ever message over the telegraph was sent on 24 May 1844 by Morse. It was a passage from the Bible's Book of Numbers and read "What hath God wrought!"

Try this!

Take two tin cans and a string, and make a telephone with the help of your parents. When done, place a can against your friend's ear while you talk directly into the other can. Can you hear each other?

How did the Box Telephone work?

The Box Telephone was invented by Alexander Graham Bell in 1876–1877. It was made of a wooden frame that had two electromagnets, wire terminals, a horseshoe magnet and a trumpet-shaped receiver. The receiver worked as, both, a mouthpiece and an earpiece. When someone spoke into the mouthpiece, it made the electromagnets vibrate. These vibrations turned into electric signals which were taken from and sent to another telephone by wires attached on the two terminals.

How was electricity discovered?

Electricity is a form of energy which occurs naturally. It is said to have been discovered in 1752 by Benjamin Franklin. He conducted an experiment in order to show that lightning was electricity. He tied a metal key to a kite string and flew it during a thunderstorm to conduct electricity. Electricity from the storm clouds transferred to the metal key and flowed down the string!

Try this!

Be an energy saver! Every day, practice at least five ways to save electricity at home and school.

Pocket fact

The first power plant!
The first power plant, Pearl Street Power Station, built by Thomas Edison became operative in the year 1882.

How did the first electric light look like?

It looked quite similar to a lantern! The first electric light was made in 1800 by an English scientist Humphry Davy. He attached a charcoal strip between the ends of two wires and connected the other ends of the wires to a battery. This charged the charcoal strip and made the carbon glow. Thus, the first arc lamp was invented.

How good were the first trains?

They were much-like present-day wagons! Railways existed long before the invention of the steam engine. They were used in European mines to move heavy wagonloads of coal along tunnels. The wagons first ran on parallel wooden planks and then on iron rails. They were pulled by horses or people.

Pocket fact

Sorry for the delay!
In Japan, any train delays, over 5 minutes, usually incur an apology and a "delay certificate" for the passengers on their way to work.

Find out

At what altitude does an airplane fly?

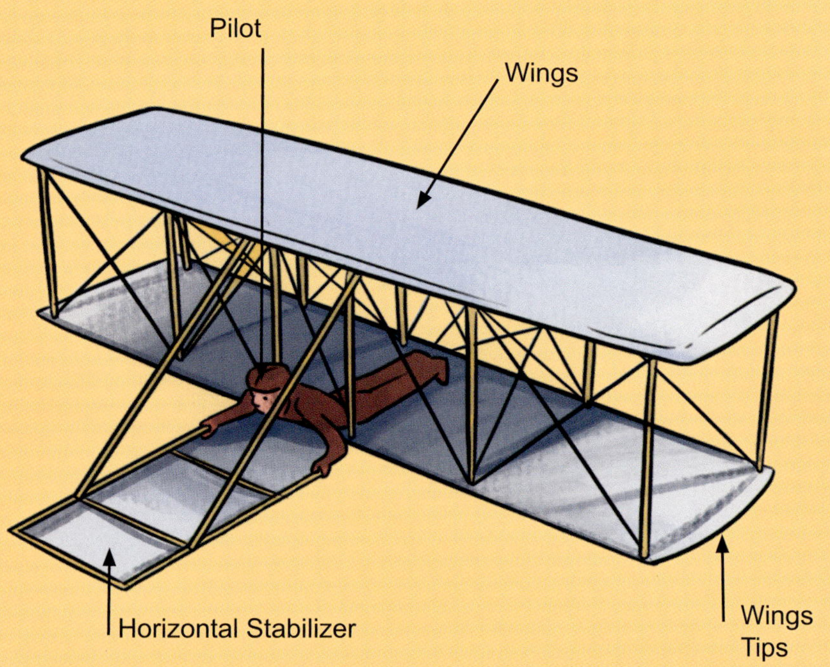

How was the first airplane different from modern airplanes?

It had many differences! The first airplane was invented by the Wright brothers in 1903. It was made of wood or canvas materials and had warped light-weight wings. Its elevators were located on the front of the aircraft. On the other hand, modern airplanes are made of aluminium. They have ailerons on their wings to control the roll of the aircraft. Their elevators are located at the tail-end of the aircraft. Modern airplanes have a cockpit with high technological controls that the first airplane lacked.

How did the early televisions work?

They displayed only black and white pictures! The first television was invented by Scottish inventor John Logie Baird. Later a Russian-American inventor Vladimir Zworykin used the cathode-ray tube (a device used to show images on a screen) in a new type of electrical television. Early televisions had huge boxes and much smaller screens. They only showed black and white pictures.

Find out

What is the full form of LED?

Pocket fact

I coined it!

The word "television" was introduced in the English language in 1907. It was coined by the Russian scientist, Constantin Perskyi.

How are LED televisions different from cathode-ray tube televisions?

They used LEDs to display images! LED televisions have small LEDs behind the screen that produce high-quality images with vibrant colours. Due to the use of LEDs, the screen is power efficient and much slimmer in size. On the other hand, cathode-ray tube TVs have a cathode-ray tube that displays the image on the screen. They are large in size and have wide viewing angles.

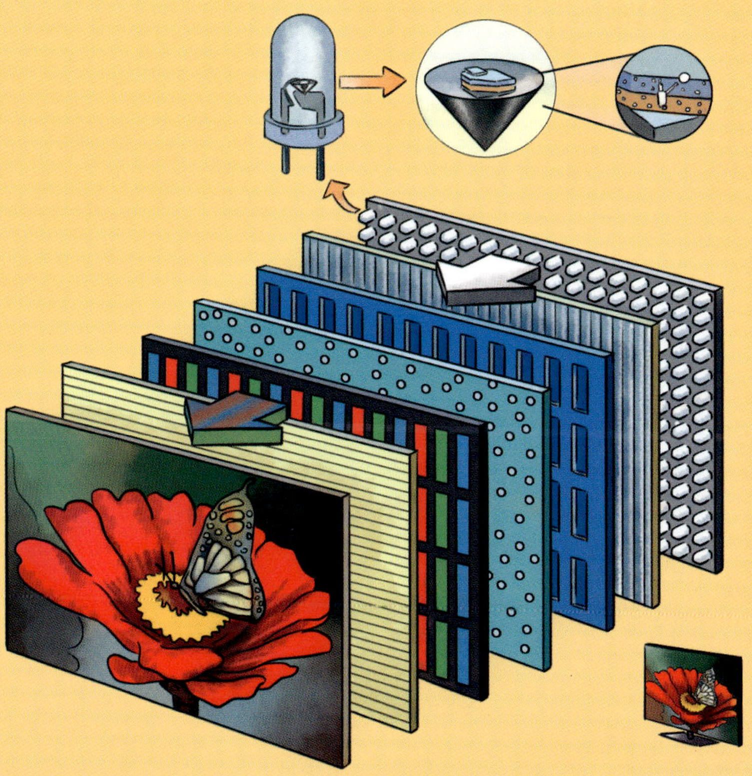

How did the first computer look like?

It was huge and complicated! The Analytical Engine is generally considered the first computer. It was invented by Charles Babbage in the early 19th century. It had four main parts that are the essential components of every computer today. The mill was the calculating unit (CPU in a modern computer), the store was where data were held prior to processing (memory in a modern computer) and the reader and printer were the input and output devices.

Try it!

Compare the keys of a typewriter and a keyboard. List the differences.

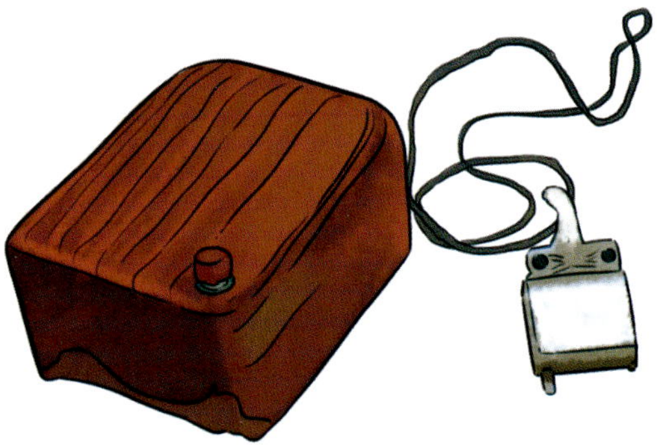

Pocket fact

ENIAC!

The first electronic computer was called the ENIAC. It weighed more than 27 tons and measured 1800 square feet.

How was the first typewriter different from the modern one?

It typed only in capital letters! The first typewriter called the Sholes and Glidden was invented by Christopher Latham Sholes. This typewriter typed only in capital letters. Its keyboard was designed to separate frequently-used pairs of type-bars so that they would not clash and get stuck at the printing point. It was a decorative machine with painted flowers and decals, and looked much like a sewing machine!

How did the idea of QWERTY keyboard evolve?

It was invented due to the keys getting jammed! The QWERTY arrangement on a keyboard was designed in 1868 by Christopher Sholes, the inventor of the typewriter. The first keyboard had keys arranged in an alphabetical order, but people typed so fast that the keys got jammed. To solve this, the keys were randomly positioned so that it could slow down the typing speed and prevent key jams.

Find out

What is the use of the pause key on the keyboard?

Pocket fact

Shortest in Japan!
The longest key on every keyboard is the spacebar. But in Japan, the statistical spacebar is much shorter than anywhere else in the world.

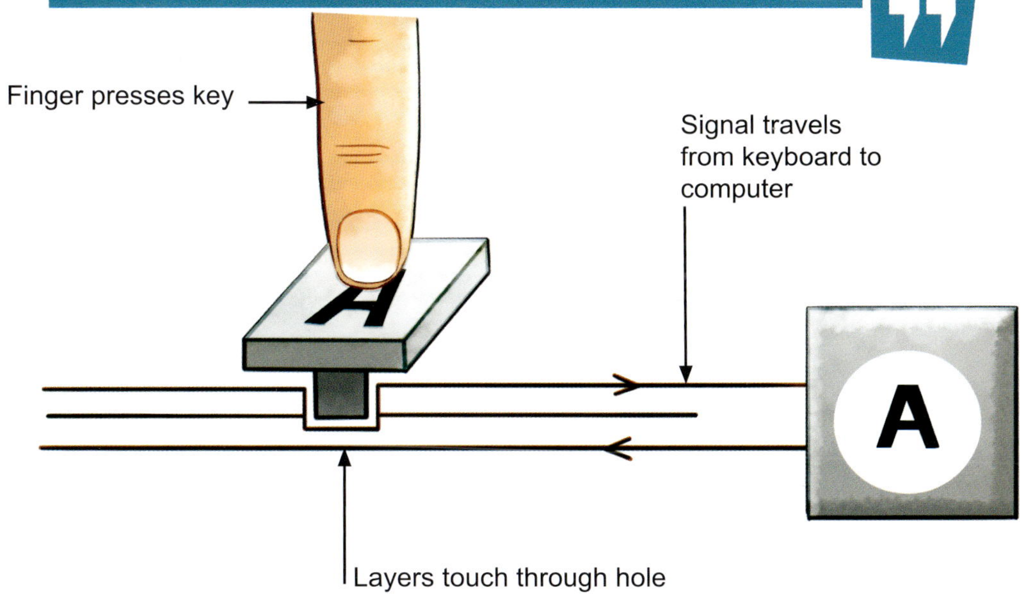

How does the keyboard put words on your screen?

It works with the help of mechanical switches! The keyboard contains its own internal processor that receives electrical signals through key strokes. Each key has a special shaped arrangement at the bottom, known as the plunger. When you press a key, an electrical signal is sent to the keyboard's internal processor. The key which is pressed is detected and letter is typed on the screen!

How did the first telescope look like?

It was a simple arrangement of lenses! The first telescope was invented in 1608 by a Dutch spectacle-maker Hans Lippershey. He fitted two small lenses in a long tube. This is how the first telescope was made. In 1609, Galileo Galilei improved this telescope. Galileo's telescope was only about 47 inches long. It had an eyepiece that provided an upright image.

Pocket fact

Look and see!
The word telescope was derived from the Greek words 'tele' and 'scope,' meaning 'far' and 'to look and see'.

Find out

What is the length of a space shuttle?

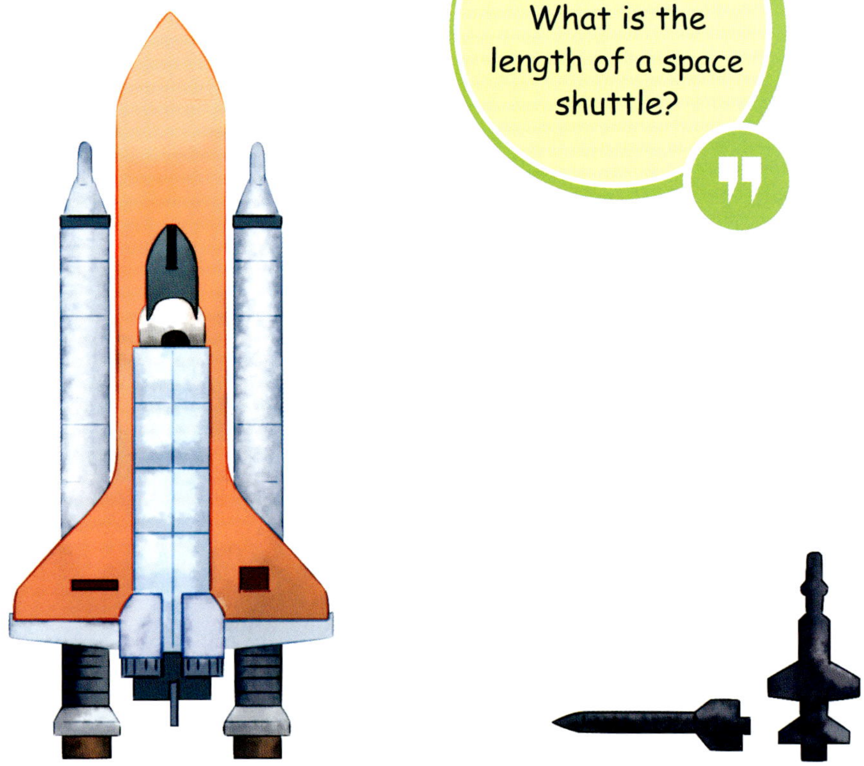

How did the first space shuttle launch and land?

It launched like a rocket but landed like a glider airplane! The space shuttle was launched by NASA. It had solid rocket boosters and main engines (on the orbiter) that helped the shuttle blast off from Earth like a rocket. The two boosters dropped off the shuttle 2 minutes after the launch and fell into the ocean. The shuttle orbiter returned to Earth like an airplane, with wheels coming out from underneath its orbiter. It rolled to a stop on a runway.

How did the compass come into being?

Find out

What was GPS earlier called?

It was inspired from the fortune tellers! The compass was invented by the Chinese. Chinese fortune tellers used a mineral called lodestone to construct their fortune-telling boards. The mineral consisted of an iron oxide which aligns itself in a north-south direction. Eventually, it was noticed that the lodestones pointed out real directions. This led to the creation of the first compass. It was made on a square slab, a lodestone spoon-shaped device that would always point south.

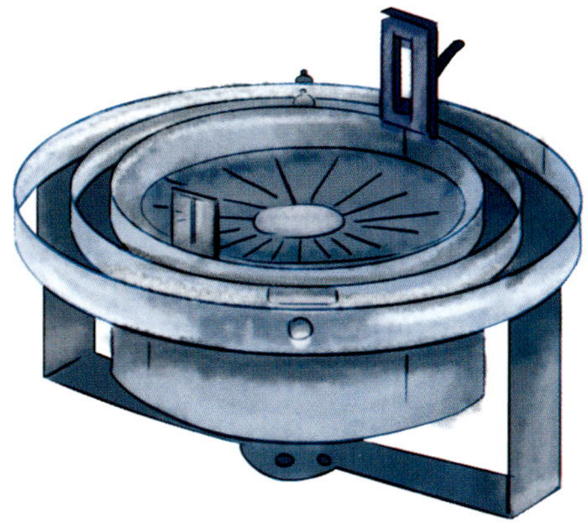

Pocket fact

That's like a tadpole!

The first needle of an iron needle compass was invented in China. It was shaped like a tadpole.

How old is the GPS system?

It started in 1957! The idea of GPS started with the satellite Sputnik. US scientists working at MIT noticed that the frequency of the radio signals transmitted by the Russian satellite Sputnik increased as it approached and decreased as it moved away. This gave them the idea to track satellites from the ground by measuring the frequency of the radio signals they emitted. This could also be used to track the location of receivers on the ground from the satellites.

Index